1

Amy Orr-Ewing

Is the Training Director of the Zacharias Trust and Programme Director for the Oxford Centre for Christian Apologetics. She is an international speaker and author, as well as being mother to 3 boys.

Frog Orr-Ewing.

Is Rector of the Latimer Minster and Chaplain and Missioner to the Oxford Centre for Christian Apologetics. He is a leadership coach, a conference speaker and an author.

millennials

REACHING AND RELEASING
THE RISING GENERATION

Amy Orr-Ewing
Frog Orr-Ewing

For Zachary, Elijah and Benjamin Orr-Ewing

Acknowledgements

A huge debt of thanks goes to Al and Libby Zadig of Charleston for your generosity and hospitality in the summer of 2009 and to Bishop Mark of South Carolina for the loan of the Bishop's Cottage. Thank you to our dear friend and research assistant Amy Yearwood for all of you efforts. Thank you to Mike and Sally Breen and the 3DM team who have encouraged us to crack on with getting these thoughts out there. Thank you to the New Wine Venue 2 team 2009 you are Millennial legends. Thank you to Xanthe and Kelvin for unforgettable hospitality in Cape Town. Thank you to Paul Capleton – you know how much you helped us. Thank you to Zachary, Elijah and Benjamin – you are the best boys in the world.

CONTENTS

INTRODUCTION

A few years ago we (Frog and Amy) were invited to take a leadership role in one of the large national Christian summer conferences in Britain and we found ourselves setting forward a vision for Deep Church. This was the beginning of a really significant journey for us, some of which we have written about in our book "Deep". We were overwhelmed by the response to that teaching and continued to build on it. However we slowly recognized that what we were doing and the way we were doing it represented quite a significant culture shift from what had gone before. The differences were not primarily theological. As we have researched and reflected on this further we have discovered that a new generation is arising in the West called the Millennials/Generation Y/ the New Victorians and that what we were doing instinctively had massively chimed with them. The Millennials love intensity, conviction, truth, passion, friendliness, holiness/rules, safety, old people, justice and inclusion.

It was not only at national gatherings of Christians that we noticed changes. After several years of leadership in a local London church we began to swap notes with other younger leaders as we started to notice a new kind of conflict – a tussle over style and vision. Interestingly this struggle appears to have been largely a clash of cultures between Generation X and the Millennials. Realising this has helped the scales fall from our eyes and encouraged us to find strategies of keeping the generations together whilst being clear on the vision of the church and holding on to what God has called us to do.

This book comes out of our journey of leadership as we are seeking to make a way for the Millennials to flourish and grow. This is important for us since they have comprised well over half of our congregation and local community. But we have come to believe passionately that it is time for us as a London church to think about this rising generation – how best to reach and release them. We are asking ourselves the question: are we standing on the cusp of a hugely significant culture shift – inside and outside the church? Are we prepared and ready to usher in God's Kingdom at such a time as this?

Millennials as the New Victorians
The Generation known as Millennials or Generation Y is comprised of those born between 1975 and 1994. They are arriving in our universities, workplaces and churches with a

markedly different approach to life, faith, work, worldview and ministry from those who precede them - namely Generation X who are now in their late thirties to early fifties.

At present a small handful of congregations are experiencing successful ministry with this generation but as a wider church we need to take seriously the culture shift which is taking place all around us and embrace the opportunities we are being presented with.

We believe that God is calling us as a national church to motivate and reach this generation and begin to establish a vibrant and effective missionary spirituality which is relevant, intriguing and challenging to the "New Victorians."

Responding to this emerging situation is crucial to the lifeblood of the Church for the next 30 years and this book aims to explore how we can do to just that in a way that is intellectually robust, spiritually rooted, historically aware, practically compassionate and authentically diverse.

The Millennials in Britain are emerging into adulthood and the job market with huge debt and social inequality, with different expectations and ways of operating than those they follow.

They have deeply held convictions, they hope for a better world and desire to rebuild the broken institutions of society - the economy, the family, the community, government and the church.

They value friendship networks, are technologically advanced and want to change the world. They are acutely aware of poverty, environmental and social justice issues, and need no persuading that these are important, and they have some of the highest levels of volunteering and activism in the country.

Within the UK Christian community many within this generation have grown up in Evangelical and Charismatic churches, often attending and helping with Soul Survivor and mission projects. This means that unlike their predecessors by the age of 25 they may have been involved in active mission projects, participated in outward-focussed youth groups, 'soulinthecity' and The Noise and may possibly have run youth and student cells for a decade. In the United States they emerged into adulthood with pledges of abstinence, a passion for justice, and a determination to pray in public places. The other side of the Millennial coin are those identified as victims of broken homes and reconstituted families, sexually active at a young age, with substance abuse and low social and educational mobility.

Taken together the New Victorians in some ways reflect the social and aspirational inequalities of their Victorian forebears which is why the label has such resonance. This generation have within them the potential to entrepreneurialism, great thinking and great achievements as the Victorians did and this is all set within the context of an acute awareness of poverty issues and brokenness.

In contrast Generation X (now aged 36-50) can be characterised within the church by a love for deconstruction, community/small groups, discursive learning styles, a desire to shock and push the boundaries, detachment, and irony. They are allergic to rules, tradition, conformism and legalism. Their use of edgy language and challenging of religiosity have become par for the course in many churches – those who were once the rebels are now the guardians of the status quo.

Unlike the disillusioned post-moderns of Generation X, the Millennials dare to believe. They need to be led, encouraged and harnessed, and they need strong and hopeful churches who can be focal points for them to gather in order to go.

The following pages are not intended to encapsulate any sort of definitive overview, but, are instead offered as tentative insights into the mentality of those we love and minister to and so are presented as reflections which we hope will help others on a similar journey.

During 2009, on a sabbatical in South Carolina, where we were the guests of generous friends in Charleston we were given the space to reflect on almost 10 years of fruitful yet tiring ministry amongst sceptics and Christians. We digested many of our mistakes and recorded some of our discoveries from ministry in Oxford, London and around the world. Amy is an apologist, author, evangelist and lecturer; Frog has been associate and then senior pastor (vicar) of two congregations over that time. In the year since then, we have read and digested web and written commentaries, analysed statistical data from the USA and the UK, carried out extensive interviews and checked our findings with leaders in the field. Amy Yearwood, our own researcher, a Millennial herself, has been an enormous help as we have sifted through analysis especially from the UK, USA, Europe and Australia.

As a new decade begins it is important to remember that seasons come and go, generations rise and fall, but the church is called to always be there reaching and connecting – ever listening to a changing world whilst offering an unchanging message of an Eternal Saviour. This reality of change and flux unsettles the desire for comfort and the status quo, filling some with a sense of unease. It is ironic that those who embrace the changes necessary to meet one generation's challenges often find it hardest to adapt afresh.

May we rise to the opportunities before us with faithfulness and courage.

CHAPTER 1

What the Commentators are Saying

The rise of post modernity and the strength of Generation X in influencing society and the church with their cultural preferences has lulled many of us into a sense that these things are what "young people want." However – in reality Gen X are now in their forties and fifties and despite being used to calling the changes and setting the tone for what is 'in vogue', 'cutting edge' and 'culturally relevant', a new very different set of attitudes is emerging. This has taken many commentators by surprise – and in the church we are only at the very beginning of waking up to the possibilities and challenges that the Millennials or New Victorians are presenting us with. Even the Millennials are themselves being overtaken by the teenagers sometimes referred to as 'iGen' – named after those who have been brought up in the era of the ipod, the iphone and the ipad.

Sociologists do not really agree on when the Millennial generation begins and ends and so commentators also vary in their perceptions of who we are actually talking about. But a broad approach would be to say that the Millennials are those born between 1975 and 1994, whereas others use 1980 as a convenient cut-off point. These rising generations' young adults appear to share a few prominent characteristics which provide a helpful starting point for us in understanding who they are, what makes them tick, and the kind of churches we can expect them to build. Strauss and Howe introduce the idea of Generations: *"History creates generations, and generations create history. The cycle draws forward energy from each generation's need to redefine the social role of each new phase of life it enters. And it draws circular energy from each generation's tendency to fill perceived gaps and to correct (indeed, overcorrect) the excesses of its elders."* [1]

We have used the term 'New Victorians' to emphasise that there are two sides to the story of the rising generations, neither of which is mutually exclusive. There are those who are enfranchised, the affluent, empowered young adults bolstered by self-esteem, and those who have unravelled even further than their parents, concentrated around new urban realities with a greater divide between rich and poor, and less social mobility than their parents grew up with.

---

1   http://www.fourthturning.com/html/about_our_message.html

The Millennials/New Victorians are technologically competent, they have never known life without email, mobile phones and the internet. They are the initiators of social networking sites such as Facebook and feel comfortable with the constant change and progression of technology. We must not underestimate the significance of this as it represents not just a difference in technological competence but more importantly a difference in mentality. The capacity to think visually and process digital imagery with razor sharp discernment leads to subtle and complex ways of accessing and sharing information.

And the New Victorians (both the empowered and the neglected) are the children of a drug and sexual revolution. Many have parents no longer together, have been brought up in reconstituted families, and have entered adulthood with a fragility which needs to be understood – straddling a wider and wider gap between their lived, felt and experienced lives and those which they long for, aspire to and expect.

"This is a time of soaring expectations and crushing realities". Joan Chiaramonte, head of the Roper Youth Report, who says that for young people "the gap between what they have and what they want has never been greater."[2]

Howe and Strauss agree, citing that "By the standard measure of American life, the Millennials children of immigrant parents face daunting challenges. A third of them live below the poverty line. A third of them have no health insurance. Three in five immigrant children (and two in five second-generation–immigrant children) live in overcrowded housing."[3]

Though their parents split up, they want to stay together, though they may have had one-night stands and lost their virginity in their early teens, they hunger for romance, though they have taken drugs and binge drink, they want to get through their rebellion by their early twenties. Many have been brought up with a scientific worldview, but believe in supernatural creation, have a spirituality but not a clear faith, have loneliness and an obsession with friendship.

The New Victorians use technology to find their social balance, community is important and is maintained electronically (although rarely initiated this way) – which means that they know where to place themselves and their

2   Twenge, Generation Me, p.2
3   Strauss and Howe, Millennials Rising, p.84

communities within national and global networks and cultures. They exist in multiple parallel communities- ethnic, cultural and global. They have debt and expectations of wealth, fame and celebrity, but have not yet mastered a realistic way of getting there.

They have heartache and they have hope.

Celebrity and Brands

"… Consumerism is arguably *the* religion of the late twentieth (now early twenty-first century).'" Steve Miles, *Consumerism as a Way of Life*, Sage, 1998.

"The only values that have been propagated in the place of traditional structures are those of brands, logos and celebrity. Having built their entire identity around these, young people need them more than ever." Simon Guild, MTV 2005

"Younger people tend to be more brand-driven as they are more inexperienced consumers, using a brand as a shortcut to choosing the right product. The paradox is they also use brands to express their individuality. With product preferences as yet un-rooted in consistent shopping behaviour, young consumers are more likely to try out different brands." (nVision Research)

The Rising generations love celebrity, stardom and brands. Fame is its own achievement. The age of reality TV has given way to the resurgence in talent shows so beloved of the early days of television and revived for the texting, downloading, Youtubing generation. It has become more important to be famous than to be talented, to be a celebrity than to be qualified, to be rich than to be deserving.

Bemused by the New Victorians...

'Often parents don't realize that their sexual revolution has become the entrenched status quo.'[4]

Though by no means universal there is also a strange thing developing in the area of conformity, which affects their shopping habits, cultural and technological preferences and their morality. This is in itself a partial rejection of the obsession with rebellion, deconstruction and difference that established a cynical backdrop to GenX. If emerging generations often reject the culture of those who go before them, then two opposing instincts might naturally assert themselves. Either when faced with the 'permissive' generation children could push the envelope further and earlier than those who have preceded them, or they could rebel by

---

4   Shalit, Op Cit. p.7

rejecting certain aspects of permissiveness.

This can be seen on both sides of the Atlantic, especially in our urban centres – both the Observer in New York and the Telegraph from London have featured bemused columns chronicling a new reality:

"There was a time, not too long ago, when the young and the aimless hightailed it to New York City in pursuit of an altogether different urban experience than the domestic bliss enjoyed by Miss Miller and many of her bosom companions. High on a cocktail of recklessness and abandon, they came here to find their id, lose their superego, shake up the world, or simply shake their thang. Then they promptly chronicled these exploits in confessional sex columns.

But recent years have seen a breed of ambitious, twentysomething nesters settling in the city, embracing the comforts of hearth and home with all the fervor of characters in Middlemarch. This prudish pack—call them the New Victorians—appears to have little interest in the prolonged puberty of earlier generations. While their forbears flitted away their 20's in a haze of booze, Bolivian marching powder, and bed-hopping, New Vics throw dinner parties, tend to pedigreed pets, practice earnest monogamy, and affect an air of complacent careerism."[5]

---

5   http://www.observer.com/2007/new-victorians

Bryony Gordon in London, writes:

"The New Victorians are an emerging breed of people in their twenties who resist the popular conventions of binge-drinking and picking up debt and sexually transmitted diseases in favour of a more traditional, homely lifestyle. People like Kate are more interested in growing carrots than sniffing cocaine. They would rather sew than shop. They won't be spotted at the Sloane nightspot Boujis; the only club they go to is the book one. They're rebels, but not as we know it. Nonconformists who, well, conform. Kate says: *'I think that we all grow up so quickly nowadays and I got all the debauchery out of my system in my late teens. I'm not madly into going out, though that's not to say I don't. We'd just rather nest and cook.'* Where are the 7am finishes after drug-fuelled nights in cool East End clubs? Where are the gruelling careers? Where is the twentysomething, Sex and the City-style glamour? When, exactly, did it become cool to be so uncool?"

When it comes to relationships they also crave security and more traditional values. Many have watched their own parents divorce – but this does not put them off monogamy as we might imagine. As Bryony Gordon discovers:

"When Jacqui Spence was 11 years old her parents went through an acrimonious divorce. Now 25, she says that, rather than put her off marriage, it has convinced her of the need to really work at it. Next year she will marry her boyfriend of three years. 'It [her parents' divorce] was such a mess that it's given me this sense of the importance of kids being brought up in a protected environment,' says Spence, who has just had her bathroom redone and will soon start on the kitchen in her east London home. 'I look at my grandparents and they're still happily married. I mean, their generation would never have conceived of getting a divorce, but my parents' generation seems to have found marriage so disposable. I'm not going to make their mistakes.'"

William Strauss, a generation historian comments: "These are the kids of the baby boomers, who were all about individualism. Children tend to correct the mistakes of their parents – youth culture is defined by adults in that way – and so what we are seeing now is a product of them being uncomfortable with how important self-exploration has become. There's a sense of needing to find a balance between community and the individual, the latter being too strong and the former being too weak. There's a push towards having more decorum.

There's every sign that this generation has more of a civic instinct. I think they will create new mores, because they feel that their parents' obsession with individualism has vanquished them."

This can also be seen elsewhere in Europe, in a story that was picked up all over the world, and resonated widely:

"Forty years after their mothers and grandmothers first claimed the right to flaunt their femininity, today's young women have discovered what has been dubbed "la nouvelle pudeur" – new modesty. The cultural shift is being put down to a backlash against the liberal ideas of previous generations. French commentators have now declared that the days of the proudly-held bosom, the monokini and the no-strap tan may be over."

"It's the most eye-catching summer trend: female holiday-makers who go in for topless sunbathing on our beaches are fewer and fewer in number," said Le Parisien newspaper. "Some have decided to put their tops back on. Others – especially the younger generation – have never dreamed for a minute of trying out the monokini experience."

"At one private beach at Bormes-les-Momosas on the Mediterranean coast, fewer than two per cent were topless this week. "It used to be about half," said one sunbather in her 40s. The women's magazine Elle noted the return of a value – la pudeur – which it thought "had been put firmly in the discarded goods cupboard since May 1968".

According to a recent poll by the IFOP agency, 88 per cent of French women describe themselves as pudiques. Nearly half say they are shocked by the sight of bare breasts on a beach, and 57 per cent by bare breasts in the garden.
The most striking finding was that younger women are far more unwilling to bare all than their mothers or grandmothers. A quarter of 18 to 24 year-olds even described themselves as "tres pudiques". Jean-Claude Kauffman, a sociologist said it was a sign of less showy times. "We are witnessing a return to more safety and family-oriented values. Modesty and discretion are the order of the day," he said.[6]

Despite the growing reality of some young adults and teenagers increasingly rejecting the permissiveness of the previous youth revolutions, there is a vehemence in the reaction

---

6 [By Henry Samuel in Paris Published: 7:09PM BST 22 Jul
   2009.- (23/07/09)
   http://www.telegraph.co.uk/news/worldnews/europe/france/5
   887753/Modest-young-French-women-refuse-to-go-
   topless.html] ; also,
   http://www.time.com/time/world/article/0,8599,1912685,00.
   html

against modesty from the Boomers and Generation X! One author, Wendy Shalit, having written a book charting and encouraging a new modesty came in for some startling responses from both sides:

"Although we live in a supposedly liberated age, our hysterical witch-hunting of those who question our ideal of recreational sex suggests something else: that our liberation does not extend quite as far as we imagine. But I wasn't discouraged, not even when I received death threats, because I was too busy reading fascinating letters from young women. Precisely because being a romantic is nowadays an unpardonable sin, these young women, thousands of them, had been sure that something was very wrong with them. and it never fails to touch me. Here is an excerpt from Rachel: *You basically laid out almost exactly how I felt as a woman. I am twenty years old and have been asking myself questions like, "What's wrong with me? Why haven't I had sex yet?" . . . Anyway, reading your book, my faith was restored. I am a romantic. . . . I couldn't figure out why I hadn't just slept with this guy or that one like my friends do. And I'll say I was so close to doing that just because I thought it would help me grow up. Be more my own age. Even my mother wanted me to do it. And that's why I thank God I read your book when I did. I began crying toward the end when I realized that nothing was wrong with me and that I was lucky to still have what I have. My desire to be with one person isn't childish or immature. . . . I'm not scared; I just don't have an interest in [sex] as a sport. [7]"*

Elle magazine's French edition felt it necessary to urge their older readers not to be depressed or appalled by the younger girls refusal to bare all – explaining that the feminism battle of another generation had won the rights, and now they had to respect the choices. This was no longer a liberation struggle, but a lifestyle choice. Girls are increasingly regretting the sexual and moral decisions they have made as teenagers and may already be moving towards conformity by their twenties.[8]

So this is a generation who in the 1990's got on board with the 'silver ring thing', the abstinence and 'true love can wait' campaigns, accompanied with the WWJD (what would Jesus do) wrist-bands. At one stage the WWJD website was receiving over 2 million hits and comments per month. While they may not have succeeded in actually changing sexual practice by turning round the trends in teenage pregnancies or reducing STD's, they do seem to have struck a

---

7   Shalit, Wendy. The Good Girl Revolution. (Ballantine, 2008 p.6) see also http://blogs.modestlyyours.net/

8   http://archpedi.ama-assn.org/cgi/content/abstract/160/6/591 41% of teenage girls interviewed had unwanted sex

chord, and they did send out some sort of a message. In other words though some studies seem to suggest that abstinence programmes may not have been that successful, and while GenX seem happy to comment on the failure and the danger of repressing sexual urges, many of those who didn't manage to keep their pledge of waiting are miserable, because *they wanted to* and they regret the fall from early idealism.[9]

The 1990's and early 00's witnessed a surge amongst Christian young people, at least, of wanting to assert their right not to be sexualised, but later found they were not really up to the task of purity. However, many are taking the opportunity to settle and marry nevertheless having got over their experimentation by their twenties.

---

9   http://www.timesonline.co.uk/tol/news/uk/article1971937.ece also http://www.silverringthing.org.uk much criticism of abstinence movements have centred on 'failure rate' http://www.washingtonpost.com/wp-dyn/content/article/2008/12/28/AR2008122801588.html citing Janet E Rosenbaum. Reborn a virgin: Adolescents' retracting of virginity pledges and sexual histories. American Journal of Public Health. 2006; 96:1098–1103 tp://ajph.aphapublications.org/cgi/reprint/96/6/1098.pdf "In an NBC/*People* poll, almost half of young teens said that their sexual contact was outside of a relationship." Twenge, *Gen Me, p.168*

Technology

"According to Nielsen Mobile, in the first quarter of 2009, the average U.S. teen made and received an average of 191 phone calls and sent and received 2,899 text messages per month. By the third quarter, the number of texts had jumped to a whopping 3,146 messages per month, which equals more than 10 texts per every waking non-school hour. (At the beginning of 2007, those numbers were 255 phone calls and 435 text messages.) Preteens sent and received 1,146 texts per month."[10]

One thing you can usually rely upon is that parents are sometimes befuddled by their children, and nowhere is this more true than in the realm of technology. We will address this again later, but it is safe to say the increasing use and development of communications technology is leaving some incredulity:

Larry Rosen is a professor of psychology at California State University, wrote an article for CNN in Feb 2010: *"I tried to reach my teenage daughter the other day. I left a voice mail, sent an e-mail message and finally texted her and told her to check both and call me back. Seconds later, she texted back one letter: "K." She is 19 and has been sending and receiving upwards of 3,000 texts per month. One*

---

10 *[http://edition.cnn.com/2010/OPINION/02/08/rosen.texting.co mmunication.teens/]*

month, she hit 7,500! She is not unusual at all.[11]

Now there are many young people who are not such text addicts, but the area of technology and communication is something which is signalling a significant shift from the Generation X and those coming after them. Once information technology was cool, but now it is part of the fabric of life, existence and communication. "Millennials assume they have unlimited and free (or virtually free) access to information. For them, the Internet has the affect of obliterating boundaries between what can and cannot be known."[12]

Before we can assess whether this is a good or bad thing – whether the ever-constant use of technology in media is neutral, damaging or enhancing, it is important to register that a fundamental and possibly irreversible change has occurred – the trend has reached tipping point.

Thomas de Zengotita[13] is amongst those who point to possible 'technococoons' – an environment shaped and lived from the confines of a bedroom or study – from which much

---

11 *Op Cit. see also http://www.usatoday.com/news/health/2010-02-10-igeneration10_CV_N.htm; http://www.usatoday.com/news/education/2010-02-24-millennials24_ST_N.htm obref=obinsite,*

12 Greenberg, *Gen We,* p.94

13 Zengotita, *Mediated,* p.ix,

relating operates 'virtually'. Whilst there are vast swathes of the global population for whom such 'wired-up' existence is economically unattainable. There are trends which are reaching globally amongst the economically franchised. The pace of change, the hours spent accessing and using new media, and the instance of multi-tasking is also different.

It is said that once a technology is being used by 50 million people, it is said to have penetrated society. Radio took nearly 40 years to reach this impact, the telephone about 20 years, TV and mobile phones about 15 years. MySpace and Facebook were unknowns in 2003 and now have several hundred million users. Youtube was being used by 50 million consumers in a single year.

Language is being affected – new words coined regularly, twittering and tweets, IM'ing, texting, iphone, Wii, malware, google, blog. We could even now ask – 'have you GPS'ed or googlemapped your directions?' 10 years ago that sentence would have been nonsense.

The hours spent using this technology is also massively on the rise, with American teenagers spending up to 21 hours a day using the new media. They are doing this by simultaneous multi-tasking or hypertasking, sometimes when in leisure, sometimes at work – sitting in lectures whilst texting. Uploading videos whilst listening to music, browsing the web, watching TV in the background and with a single earpiece in to listen to music and the other ear open to the world! Children and early teens are not far behind, averaging nearly 10 hours a day.[14]

Brands and Reality

Millennials are not worried by 'brands', in fact, they like them, and they gain trust and confidence from known brands in a bewilderingly over-complex environment. Whilst the local, the small and the authentic are positive things, when it comes to church a brand may become increasingly important. This is not the same as a denomination or even a dogmatic or theological position, and it is not to be confused with ideas of peddling the gospel.

A brand is an image of a product within the world, including the logo or the look, but not constrained by it. A brand is also the resonance or the pyschological effect in the mind of the consumer. The psychological aspect, sometimes referred to as the **brand image**, is a symbolic system created within the minds of people and consists of all the information and expectations associated with a product or service.

---

14 Rosen, R*ewired*, p.29.

The brand in question is 'church' or a specific stream of church, Christianity or spirituality. We are not suggesting that a single local church should have to find its place in the marketplace of ideas or trying to corner the market share in the town, but to fail to understand the importance of brands is to fail to engage at a meaningful level with younger people. Younger people are immersed in an advertful existence, they are used to being engaged with as consumers, they are becoming increasingly discerning, and able to weigh up complex visual and cultural references, get ironies and subversions, pick up on the game-playing of films and appreciate new media, viral adverts and interactive branding. Lives which are affected (or infected!) by so many layers of media (broadcasting, reality TV, airbrushing) that working out the REAL becomes problematic. From the 'real real' – you fall down the stairs, through the 'staged real' – a politician in a TV interview, past the 'edited real real' of documentaries with footage taken with hidden cameras, and ending up with 'in-between overtly and covertly unreal realistic' – a TV advert with switched footage of an actor, like Paul Newman or John Wayne driving a modern car, when one is meant to realise that though they are dead, the car is real.[15]

---

15 "Real Real: Observed Real: In-Between real real and

Millennials expect to be able to connect with a brand at various points of delivery, both in the shop and online. When it comes to church, expect both the online presence and the 'point of delivery' to be under intense scrutiny.

A very simple example of the significance of this in church life is the whole realm of the church website. Expect a New Victorian to assess what a church is trying to present about itself in approximately 3 minutes. The use of colour and imagery will speak volumes about the age profile and culture of the church, the orientation of the website to members or the general public will speak of the attitude to mission, a secretive approach to certain kinds of information raises alarm bells in a generation used to accessing data and assessing it for themselves. A vacuous website with a predominance of image and little content will speak of the value placed on preaching teaching and discipleship.

The Millennials will also read online reviews and reports about a church. Recently in researching a prominent Anglican church in Britain we were amazed to discover that 3 of the

---

observed real: Edited real real: Edited observed real: Staged real: Edited staged real: Staged observed real unique: Staged observed real repeated: staged realistic staged hyperreal overtly unreal realistic covertly unreal realistic 'in-between overtly and covertly unreal realistic' real unreal unreal real."
See also Rosen, L. *Rewired,* p 17

first 10 Google hits on the church were alarmingly negative. The church appeared to have made no attempt at rectifying this with positive strategies and we realized that the leaders were unaware of their church's *web presence.*

A church with a significant contingent of Millennials would be unlikely to find itself in this position. They would want to visit the church and find an authenticity, a link between the virtual presentation and the real. As if the online browse and the store are holding the same item, the real and the virtual real are meant to be linked. Churches have long been used to the importance of architecture, and the presence of a church within the community, on the High Street or the intersection – now the web presence and the online environment have also become important, and this is unlikely to diminish.

The Millennials will want to contribute, though, to this reality and this perception, they will not want to be just content receivers, but also content generators.

The Climb

"They are growing up in a world that feels post-truth, post-sacrifice, post-heroic, post-anything truly ennobling... Already Millennials teens are hard at work on a grassroots reconstruction of community, teamwork, and civic spirit. They're doing it in the realms of community service, race, gender relations, politics, and faith." [16]

In the USA, the Disney teen star Miley Cyrus originally performed this song, The Climb, as the lead for her movie as 'Hannah Montana', and it was the most popular audition song for American Idol. It reached double platinum and was a top ten hit on three continents. While the inspirational cross-over to Christianity was clear in the lyrics, for the UK this reference was removed in the cover version for finalist for the X Factor, Joe McEldery.

It is a good song to end the chapter on – having reached its popularity across so many media, amongst so many teens, and supported by vigorous campaigns on the web – celebrity, fame, hope, consumption and above all a positive outlook on the struggles in life – it's the climb which dignifies, not necessarily the destination or the starting point.

I can almost see it
That dream I am dreaming
But there's a voice inside my head saying
"You'll never reach it"
Every step im taking, every move I make feels
Lost with no direction, my faith is shaken

---

16 Strauss and Howe, Millennials Rising, p.214

... But I gotta keep trying
Gotta keep my head held high

There's always gonna be another mountain
I'm always gonna wanna make it move
Always gonna be a uphill battle
Sometimes I'm gonna have to lose

Ain't about how fast I get there
Ain't about what's waiting on the other side
It's the climb

...Keep on moving,
keep climbing

Keep the faith, baby
It's all about,
it's all about the climb
Keep the faith,
keep your faith, whoa[17]

---

17 Songwriters Alexander, J; Mabe, J;

CHAPTER 2

Generational Analysis

Generation Y are shaping up to be hugely significant they will rival the Boomers in sheer number as 71 million of them in the States come of age. The significance of the sheer numbers should not be underestimated nor should the magnitude of the cultural change that the mentality of the Millennials will bring in the church if we manage to reach them and in society at large.

One thing is certain and that is that we are living in a time when young adults are bringing a fresh set of hopes, dreams and way of operating to bear on the society around them. As the Millennials Gen Y'ers or New Victorians arise there is some disagreement amongst researchers as to the salient markers of this generation all of which is exacerbated by the numerical facts – this generation being so numerous and inevitably diverse. The majority of Gen Y in the West have grown up in unprecedented economic stability, which has contributed to their notable outlook of optimism – a sharp contrast with the cynicism that seemed to typify Generation X.

This chapter will look at the important trends emerging as the Millennials take their place in the adult world– even when such trends appear to be contradictory all the while trying to remember the dangers of generalisations. The optimistic hope-filled generation are also the generation of vast social inequalities, the most educated generation in the West live side by side with fellow Millennials with low literacy, poor social mobility and huge educational disadvantage. "The Millennials' first perception of the public world and the adults who run it has … been dominated by two basic elements: First, by a confident individualism, which kids see reflected both in rising personal optimism and in a booming free-market economy; and second, by a disturbing social fragmentation, which kids see reflected in the vast distance now separating persons and families – by income, race, language, and lifestyle."[18]

Huge amounts of the research that has been done on the Millennials has been commissioned by companies hoping to increase their profits. Selling to the Millennials is big business – research is necessary. In the church we are only just waking up to the need to inform ourselves about the culture of contemporary young adults, not in order to change the gospel to suit them

_____

18 *Millennials Rising,* p.98

but to become more effective at reaching out with the unchanging truth and to tackle unnecessary cultural baggage which may hinder some from considering Christ.

Millennials Rising identifies seven distinguishing traits of the Millennial persona.

o   *Special...* older generations have inculcated in Millennials the sense that they are, collectively, vital to the nation and to their parents' sense of purpose.

o   *Sheltered...* Millennials are the focus of the most sweeping youth safety movement in American history.

o   *Confident...* Millennials teens are beginning to equate good news for themselves with good news for their country.

o   *Team-oriented...* Millennials are developing strong team instincts and tight peer bonds.

o   *Achieving...* With accountability and higher school standards rising to the very top of America's political agenda, Millennials are on track to become the best-educated and best-behaved adults in the nation's history.

o   *Pressured...* Millennials feel a 'trophy kid' pressure to excel.

o   *Conventional...* Millennials support convention – the idea that social rules can help."

On the one hand the Millennials often get a bad press: "According to a national survey, barely one adult in three thinks that today's kids, once grown, will make the world a better place."[20]

But on the other hand there is a recognition amongst some leaders that the churches desperately need to address the challenge of reaching Generation Y. In a report from the Evangelical Alliance Council Meeting on September 16, 2009 on The 18-30 Mission: A Missing Generation, it was commented that: "In research carried out by Innovista it was found that 96% of church leaders think that increasing the number of 16-30 year olds in their church is either more important or as important as any other top priority. Yet despite this, only 11% of the same church leaders felt 'well resourced' to do this in terms of people, training, and tools."

One leader commented the lack of young adults in church on Sunday "is the churches' dirty little secret." This book aims to address the challenge and present some of the research that has been done by companies and sociologists in a form that is useful to leaders.

------

19 *Millennials Rising*, p.43f
20 Ibid, p.3

Work

Gen Y'ers are very ambitious but not always realistic about the real world of work. They want rapid vocational progress, are comfortable with speed and change, and need constant feedback in the workplace. In general they are less loyal to a workplace than previous generations. They are looking for a job that will give them everything.

Gen Yers' career choices and behaviour are driven primarily by their quest for a chance to play meaningful roles in meaningful work that helps others. In essence they want to be "paid volunteers." The "magic" for Gen Yers comes in making a difference -producing something worthwhile- whilst working with a great team and getting the rewards they feel they deserve. At the same time unemployment is an increasing factor for many Millennials. Unemployment among young people has risen to a level not seen since the early 90s. Some 928,000 people ages between 16 and 25 were out of work in the UK in the three months to June 2009, up from a low of 521,000 in April, 2001. [21]

Millennials have very high expectations of the world of work. Fourteen common expectations of Gen Y have been identified: "Provide

21 EAUK Survey

challenging work that really matters, balance clearly delegated assignments with freedom and flexibility, offer increasing responsibility as a reward for accomplishments, spend time getting to know staff members and their capabilities, provide ongoing training and learning opportunities, establish mentoring relationships, create a comfortable low-stress environment, allow some flexibility in scheduling, focus on work but be personable and have a sense of humour, balance the role of boss and team player, treat Y'ers as colleagues not as interns or teenagers, be respectful and call forth respect in return, consistently provide constructive feedback, reward Yers when they've done a good job."[22]

What does this mean for the church?
Ministry amongst the unemployed will be vital as will a Christian mandate to entrepreneurship. Inspired minds creating businesses which will provide employment should be a Christian ideal. Within the church staff teams may well experience faster turn over but will also benefit from hugely talented and inspiring individual being willing to work for little money in the church if they are rightly released and inspired.

---

22 Martin & Tulgan, *Managing Gen Y, p.63*

Money

In a broad overview, the largest portion of Millennials earns between £10,000-16,000 per year. As many as 18% have no income.

In 2008, the Average gross weekly income for men aged 22-29 was 467.10GBP, and for women aged 22-29 426.10GBP. [23]

In America the "U.S. Census Bureau report says a person holding a high school diploma makes an average of $29,448 a year, while someone with a bachelor's earns $54, 689, and those with a masters or above make $79,946." [24]

In the U.S. most studies show that up to 80% of Gen Ys believe they will be financially better off than their parents.[25]

In the U.S., a March 2001 Northwestern Mutual poll of college seniors, 73% said they thought it very likely they would be able to afford the lifestyle they grew up in; and 21% said it was somewhat likely. 37% currently own 3 or more credit cards, while only 13% claim none. [26]

---

23 EA Survey, source ASHE 2008, ONS
24 *Millennial Leaders*, p 30
25 Martin & Tulgan, *Managing Gen Y*
26 *Getting Inside Generation Y*

The fall 2000 Lifestyle and Media Student Monitor report that overall, college students today have a purchasing power of $105 billion, and that 6 out of 10 earn this money through a part-time job.[27]   In the U.S. 1 out of 9 high schoolers has a credit card co-signed by a parent. (Business Week).

"In October 2006, a poll of 18-25 year olds asked them what their most important goal was. Number 1 was 'getting rich': 81% said that was an important goal. 51% said becoming famous was an important goal. Only about 30% said helping someone who needed help, about 20% said becoming leaders in the community, and only about 10% said becoming more spiritual." [28]

What does this mean for the church?
Money is not seen as necessarily "evil" – Christian young adults may well earn significantly and need to be discipled as to the potential for investing in the Kingdom and not fearing wealth. Teaching on giving will need to be strong and clear as will the link between caring about social justice and doing something about it personally as the gap between rich and poor increases.

––––––––––––

27 Getting Inside Gen Y
28 Millennial Leaders, p11

Debt

Debt is the great unquestioned pillar of today's society even in the post credit-crunch era the credit hungry market has made it very easy to obtain credit cards. In Australia, mobile phone debt is a large factor for young people. For some, their mobile bill is their biggest expense.[29] A T-Poll survey in late March 2009 about the impact of the Credit Crunch on 18-24s concluded that they were: "More than twice as likely to have borrowed money from a friend than older age groups (12%). 11% cite the decision to put off getting married or starting a family as a direct result of the current economic climate. Their greatest fear is the risk of losing their job – 74% of under-24s are concerned about becoming unemployed."[30]

A YouGov poll in 2008 for young people's charity Rainer found that 90% of young people were in debt by the age of 21. Almost half of 18-24 year olds have owed more than £2,000. 1 in 5 have owed more than £5,000 GBP. All of this must be understood in the wider context of the broader picture. Consumer debt is now at record levels in the UK across the generations – personal lending has now reached £1.25 trillion, with an average debt per household of £50,000.

29 Huntley, p37
30 EAUK Survey

British consumers are on average twice as indebted as those in Continental Europe. The number of adults who claim to have had a serious debt problem is between 7 and 9 million. A Bank of England survey – from September 2005 by NMG of 1,923 people found that 60% of adults are in debt.

What does this mean for the church?
This scourge of debt will have a huge practical, spiritual and psychological impact on congregations and communities. Inspired ministry will be sensitive and relevant to this reality. Debt projects run by churches will be a significant missional expression of the church. Teaching on money management and giving even when in debt will be significant.

Education

In the U.S. many realize that the key to success lies in advances in learning. 90% of high school seniors expect to attend college, 70% of them expect to work in professional jobs, 70% believe that college is necessary to meet their career goals, and 40% of college freshmen expect to go on for a master's degree.
In 2004, the number of UK students at universities was 1,918,680. In 2008, there were 1,964,315. 2009 saw a 10% rise in applications

from 2008 due to the recession and a demographic anomaly. Across Britain 49.2% of women aged 17-30 have been or are currently in higher education, compared with only 37.8% of men of the same age. For white working class males the number is only 6.4%.[31]   For many Millennials the opportunities for education are unprecedented, for others they are completely disenfranchised.   This is why the "New Victorian" name has such resonance – a generation faced with incredible opportunity are also a generation marked by huge inequality.

Despite huge increases in government spending, the UK has one of the lowest levels of educational equality in the Western world. Educational inequality and low social mobility have devastating costs to individuals and communities within our country: nearly ¾ of young offenders describe their educational attainment as nil. 1 in 5 of care leavers will be unemployed by the September after they leave school. 1 in 3 young people who have been excluded from school have been involved with drug dealing. Educational inequality is driven principally by domestic factors.   Children from disadvantaged backgrounds are five times more likely to fail academically compared with their peers. The most under-achieving group is white

---

31 EAUK Survey

children from disadvantaged backgrounds – just 17% of disadvantaged white boys attain 5A*-C at GCSE. Children in Care are the lowest achieving social group and despite almost £1 billion being spent on them in the last 8 years, only 11% attain 5 good GCSEs.

What does this mean for the church?
The educational attainments of the Millennials will be great and so the churches will need to have an integrated Christian worldview which takes the life of the mind seriously. At the same time educational inequality will make it more and more important for Churches to engage with the poor – empowering the disadvantaged with an education, helping the illiterate to read – as Biblical communities have always done, but now the need for this will be here at home as well as abroad.

Consumerism and Brands

Increased globalization and competition have caused expectations of lifestyle and standards of living to rise. Due to the amount of adverts, the focus of the Millennial consumer has become lifestyle image rather than functional need. Lifestyle brands now have so much importance that it makes it harder for Millennials to live without them. The buying habits of young Millennials are likely to follow them into adulthood. Money is primarily focused on leisure, experience, and goods. They also have more money to spend then previous generations. With so much credit and cash, Millennials can afford to buy luxury now rather than save for later. "Technology and consumerism have colluded to create a world where everything was accessible. Used to not having to exert much effort, everything is done for them from online shopping, to pre-made dinners."[32]

Parents have created a generation of consumers. In Australia one commentator notes: "Growing up, Y kids influenced more than 70% of their parents' clothing and food purchases… Yers are enthusiastic and indefatigable consumers."[33] The power in the hands of the consumer has shaped and defined the Millennials – they are used to exercising this power however unconsciously and they have never known life without the subtle but pervasive influence of the marketers over them. "Y consumers are both players and pawns in a cultural, social, and economic environment where the connections between identity, desire and friendship are much more complex than older generations believe them to be. Yers are undeniably brand conscious. They are conformist in their consumption habits. They

---

32 *MTV Generations 2005*
33 Huntley, p145

are influenced by a desire to fit into the tastes and trends of their friendship group."[34]

Incredibly brand-conscious world, respond to advertisement differently than generations before them, they prefer and expect to encounter them in a variety of different places (tube, train, mobile phone). Advertising is not perceived anywhere near as negatively as in previous generations. The theory that the anti-brand movement finds little resonance amongst the young is given weight by the findings above, showing that young Europeans are less likely than their older counterparts to actively resist the advertising of big brands. We might well think here that the prevalence of young people working in marketing and advertising means that there is often a sense of rapport between those marketing and those being targeted. This is borne out by nVision Research, which revealed that those in the 15-29 age group are least likely to say that 'advertising today does not reflect my life'.

Because younger people tend to be more brand-driven they are more inexperienced consumers - using a brand as a shortcut to choosing the right product. The paradox is that they also use brands to express their individuality.

According to Alissa Quart writing in Australia,

34 Huntley, 150

author of *Branded*, Yers have 'grown up in the age of the brand', in a 'contemporary luxury economy' where brands like Nike, McDonalds, Disney, and Levi's and so on were as familiar to them as the names of their own friends and relatives. Now that Yers are young adults, brand identification is still at an all-time high and shows no sign of dropping."[35]

To become part of the inner circle a brand needs to be **trusted, agile, transparent, and engaging**. These are the illusive success-defining qualities of a brand which the Millennials connect with. However this generation do not commit long-term to particular brands: "One of the emerging truisms of Gen Y is that Yers are conscious of brands but not loyal to them. They are known for having short attention spans and don't give a second though to abandoning one brand name for another."[36]

The key values that have been propagated for the Millennials in the place of traditional structures are those of brands, logos and celebrity. Having built their identity around these, young people need them more than ever.

What does this mean for the church?
Practical teaching on following Christ will

35 Huntley, 148
36 Hutley, 151

challenge rampant consumerism. But mission to Millennials will recognize the importance of brands and known and trusted Christian "brands" such as *Alpha* will continue to be important. Churches may well benefit from being part of a known or "branded" movement – Millennials will understand the shorthand of this – the values, theology and structures being invoked may help to inspire trust and interest.

Fame/Celebrity

The popular culture within which Millennials have grown up implies that talent is not the most important thing needed to make someone significant or give a sense of identity, a few minutes of fame will do it. Fame = Happiness. Celebrity offers a tangible identity and fame is the ultimate accolade conferring significance and self-worth. Instead of a few pages in a magazine telling you what a celebrity is wearing there are now multiple magazines, channels, websites, and programs all dedicated to celebrities, and still the demand grows.

What does this mean for the church?
The church cannot accommodate all the preferences of Millennials whilst passionately following Christ. The desire for fame may well be subverted into a desire for Christian heroism.

The Millennials who hope for great things may produce great Christian heroes who exemplify compassion, courage and wonderful exploits for Christ. In evangelism, Millennials may well come to hear the testimonies and stories of those who are Christians in the public eye.

Communication

Born into a world of constant technological change, the Millennials naturally adapt to whatever is introduced. They have been constantly made aware of global events due to the widespread and rapid rate of information transfer. They have also grown up surrounded by marketing language and have been bombarded with messages targeting them. Because of this they have learnt to process information selectively and take the top line messaging.

Relationships are now developed online. Vodaphone offered free Internet by advertising social networking (MySpace, Facebook). The top three social networking sites include Facebook, Bebo, MySpace.[37] 60% of UK internet users ages 16-25 have a social networking profile. What does all this mean? One of the impacts is 'hyper-

37 Sadek Wynbek Millward Brown, *What's Next in media for the youth, UK Social Network Marketing.*

communication' (mobile phones, social networking sites, IM, Blackberry, PDA, iPhone) this leads to constant multi-tasking, and the potential for CPA (Continuous Partial Attention).[38]

One writer notes: "Today's teenagers, living as they do in a media saturated culture of choice, have become incredibly good at processing large amounts of information, very quickly without paying any attention to its meaning. To combat this media channels have evolved to communicate with them through a series of simple, ready packaged, edited, sound and image bytes".

The potential speed and imminence of communication means that Gen Y are conditioned to want technology to work for them and by inference everything else *right now*. They want to know "What value can I add today?" "What can I learn today?", "What can you offer me today?", "How will I be rewarded today?" Millennials have high expectations of technology and get impatient when it doesn't measure up. [39]

What does this mean for the church?
The website of any church is vitally important –

---

38 Pew Research, *The Ties that Bind*
39 Martin and Tulgan, *Managing Generation Y.*

it is not an "in house" thing but is open to the world. Many could venture into Christian community through this vehicle imaginatively used. Social networking provides unprecedented opportunity for discipleship as well as mission in tough communities – such as Islamic or gang culture.

Morality

As we have seen in the first chapter the New Victorians are embracing ideals in a way that Generation X find extremely puzzling. Gone are the shades of grey and the suspicion of moral certainties. Millennials are convinced of some moral truths: "Gen We is *noncynical and civic-minded*. They believe in the value of political engagement and are convinced that government can be a powerful force for good… One of the most significant findings from the GMS is Millennials' interest in and belief in collective social action. When asked about the best way to address the challenges facing the country, the leading choice by far was 'through collective social movement' (60% made that their first or second choice)."[40] This certainty does not necessarily chime with Biblical truth since it is often instinctual:

"Morality is like common sense; unless you are actively resisting it, it is not hard to know what

40 Greenberg, *Gen We,* p30

to do or to do it. The vast majority are intuitionists – that is, they believe that the know what is right and wrong by attending to the subjective feelings or intuitions that they sense within themselves when they find themselves sin various situation or facing ethical questions… The majority of emerging adults interviewed had difficulty thinking of even one example of a situation recently when they had some trouble deciding what was the morally right or wrong thing to do."[41]

However moral certainty of any kind is a huge departure from the deconstructed morality of the post modern Gen X whose only certainty appeared to be the idea that you cannot actually be certain about anything. Millennials know their own minds on moral issues around social justice issues such as people trafficking, poverty, third world debt and environmental issues. They have moral convictions but while there is a good deal of overlap and massive potential for harmony, these issues have not always been the moral focus of Evangelical Christians even if they are of huge concern to the Scriptures.

Much to the puzzlement of the anarchic tendencies within Generation X who felt strongly to deconstruct the institutions of society

41 Smith, Snell, *Souls in Transition,* p46

the New Victorians believe in their possibility for good: "Most Millennials are far more trusting than their parents about the capacity of large national institutions to do the right thing on their (and the nation's) behalf."[42] They do not share their forbears frustrations with rules and moral legalism since they have no experience of it. In the face of the moral vacuum they have been raised in Millennials instinctively resonate with moves to establish fair moral standards: "Even so, today's teens widely acknowledge that the rules they must follow are fair. They respect authority and widely support new measures to suppress disorder in the classroom or out on the street…"[43]   Neither their empathy for social justice causes nor this respect for moral authority prompt them all to gravitate towards a particular political ideology – in fact as American authors Greenberg and Webber comment:

"Speaking in broad terms, Gen We is post-ideological, post-partisan, and post-political… They are post-ideological because they are uninterested in learning about and defending the 'conservative' or 'liberal' approaches to the problems our country faces. Instead they are pragmatic, open-minded, and innovation-oriented, eager to experiment with new solutions no matter where they may come from

42 *Millennials Rising*, p175
43 *Millennials Rising*, p177

and no matter what political orientation they may be associated with. They are post-partisan because, although then lean Democratic, they are disgusted with what they perceive as the narrowness, pettiness, and stagnation that often characterize both major parties... They are post-political because they are fed up and bored with the interest-group conflicts, identity-based appeals, and power-seeking maneuvers they see as dominating the public arena... they believe that all of us – not only all Americans, but all humans around the planet – will ultimately share the same destiny, and therefore must find ways to work together for the common good."[44]

On the issue of sexual morality Gen Y appear to be quite conflicted. With very high rates of sexual promiscuity and broad social acceptance of diverse sexual and family unions, Gen Y still believe in marriages. Despite the soaring divorce rates of their parents generation the majority want to get married and have children.

"GenMe has a strong desire to have children: 75% of 2003 college freshmen named "raising a family" as an important life goal, compared to only 59% of Boomer college students in 1977." [45]

44   Greenberg, *GenWe*, p55
45 Twenge, *Generation Me*, p.215

Studies also reveal that young Americans are realistic about the durability of marriage. "Over half of the respondents say one of their biggest concerns about getting married is the possibility of divorce. 88 percent think the divorce rate in America is too high. But ironically, given their own utopian aspirations for marital bliss, 86 percent say that the high divorce rate is a result of couples focusing too much on their expectations for happiness and too little on the hard work it takes to maintain a relationship." [46]

When it comes to the rebuilding of a broken society Millennials give observers huge reason for hope: "They are growing up in a world that feels post-truth, post-sacrifice, post-heroic, post-anything truly ennobling… Already Millennials teens are hard at work on a grassroots reconstruction of community, teamwork, and civic spirit. They're doing it in the realms of community service, race, gender relations, politics, and faith."[47]

What does this mean for the church?
Morality is back on the agenda and Church leaders need to re grow their backbones. Millennials are not switched off by moral certainty as Gen X were in fact they invite debate

46 Media Central Inc.
47 *Millennials Rising,* p214

and moral opinion. When reached with the gospel Millennials have the potential to fulfill the hopes and dreams of their own generation – to rebuild the family, the institutions of society and to tackle injustice in the world. Only with Christ will these goals be attainable – but how fascinating that this generation chimes so readily with core Kingdom values.

Key events to define the generation – What has shaped the Millennials?

Any sociological study of a generation looks for key defining moments and experiences that have helped to shape and mould those within.

The following table is helpfully descriptive of the American context: [48]

THE TOP TEN FORMATIVE EXPERIENCES OF THE BABY BOOMERS	EVENTS THAT MADE THE BIGGEST IMPRESSION ON THE HIGH SCHOOL CLASS OF 2000
Women in the workplace	Columbine
Sexual revolutions of the Pill and AIDS	War in Kosovo

---

48 *Source: Yankelovich: Class of 2000 Survey (1999). Virginia statewide poll of 655 members of class of 2000, conducted for Neil Howe and William Strauss*

THE TOP TEN FORMATIVE EXPERIENCES OF THE BABY BOOMERS	EVENTS THAT MADE THE BIGGEST IMPRESSION ON THE HIGH SCHOOL CLASS OF 2000
Economic expansion of the '60s and early '70s	Oklahoma City bombing
The Space Race	Princess Di's death
Rock 'n' roll	Clinton impeachment trial
The Vietnam War	OJ Simpson trial
The oil crisis of the '70s	Rodney King riots
The stock market boom and bust of the '80s	Lewinsky scandal
Watergate	Fall of Berlin Wall
Disney	McGwire-Sosa homer derby

Within the UK we might look to the launch of MTV in 1981, the fall of the Berlin Wall in 1989, the First Gulf War, Friends from 1994, the landslide Labour victory and Blair years 1997, the death of Princess Diana, the Ian Huntley murders, 9/11, Reality TV, (Big Brother, X Factor,

Pop Idol) and the Second Gulf War?

In some ways it is too early to define how the New Victorians/Gen Y/Millennials will turn out to shape their world but we can see that they present us Christians with an opportunity and a challenge as we try to reach them for Christ. If we fail to understand them and empathise with them we will fail to reach them. If we succeed in reaching this generation for Christ they have the potential to rival the Victorians in the impact they make on the world in rebuilding the community and the family, tackling poverty and seeing massive social transformation in the face of poverty and inequality. Could they usher in another great Evangelical century?

CHAPTER 3

Models of Church and the Generations.

Laying it out there...
Understanding the way we exist as communities and generations is often seen as the domain of sociological and anthropological study, but some of the analytical tools can be very instructive of what dynamics might be at work in the congregations to which we belong, or are attempting to lead. Especially as we consider the interplay between differing cultural approaches to the church and the world 'models' and 'systems' become increasingly informative. During doctoral research I (Frog) was undertaking in London I came across these insights in congregational studies and was struck by their usefulness. I found that the concept of model helped to accurately describe the dynamics both in the history of our particular congregation over a period of 140 years as well as helping understand the present culture of the congregation.

What is a model?

Model: is less prescriptive and more a descriptive term borrowed from the sociology of culture to describe trends within congregations around shared cultural elements which incorporate theology, worship and practise: *"While it is possible to identify the particular within the culture of a group or organisation, it is also possible to identify patterns that are common across similar groups and organisations, bundles of cultural elements – ideas, symbols, programmes, habits, ritual practices – grouped together in recurring ways."* [49]

A 'model' of church therefore means the predominant approach to self-understanding and ordering in the life of any single congregation. Trends in these patterns and 'bundles' can be discerned in cultural and sociological analysis to appear in more than one local context of the church. A quick way of getting a feel for a model of church is to answer the questions 'who we are' and 'how do we do things here?' If one were to survey one hundred churches in your region, it is unlikely that you would discover one hundred completely different understandings of what it means to be a congregation. Also, you would find that many

---

49 Becker, *Congregations in Conflict*, p.11

ideas of 'who we are' and 'how we do things here' would be shared across cultures and denominations.

Becker considers that we could collect these models of church into four very broad categories. Specifically, some congregations are more of a 'family' others more 'community' while others are 'houses of worship' or 'leaders' in the wider world. To some extent each model of congregation is neutral (i.e. it is not necessarily better to be a family type of church than a community type of church) but knowing what kind of a church or congregation we are or would even like to be can be very helpful. [50]

House of Worship Model

A House of Worship considers the congregation's core tasks to include providing religious functions and a focus for life events for the community at large, especially in terms of weddings, funerals, baptisms and other occasional services in the building. Congregations which have gathered around this model would emphasise Sunday worship and religious education (especially to children), concentrating on providing uplifting worship experience week by week, with a focus on teaching which helps members and attendees

50 Ibid. p13-16

understand their heritage, doctrines and rituals. These congregations make limited demands on member loyalty or time, and members would tend to meet at services. Most decisions would be made by clergy, paid staff or committees, and a key concept for mission would be 'attractional' or 'sanctuary-based' – organising services which are accessible, and 'excellent' that would draw enquirers and people needing pastoral care.

Expect a House of Worship approach in Cathedrals and city-centre churches and in churches of between 400 to 2000. Any smaller would not generate enough of a talent pool or the resources to be able to deliver excellence in worship. Theologically, the gathered services emphasise 'encounter' with God and can be popular in the sacramental tradition, but there are a variety of approaches to teaching, which one would expect to be shorter, to allow more space for worship, liturgy and prayer. House of Worship models with the language of temple and sanctuary work well in Anglican, Catholic and Pentecostal settings. Discipleship is catechumenical – i.e. a set format of lessons leading to a life event, such as baptism, confirmation or marriage. Behaving leads to believing, which leads to belonging.

Churches with this model lost large proportions of their congregations in the second half of the twentieth century, but lately are experiencing something of a small resurgence in the UK with the growing congregations in Cathedrals and of larger charismatic and pentecostal churches with popularity increasing through immigration from Eastern Europe and Africa. Generationally this model of congregation is least popular with GenX.

Family Model

For some congregations the most important answers to 'who we are' and 'how we do things' is a model of family; a place where worship, teaching and providing close-knit and supportive relationships for members are a top priority. These are the three things that are done well, that people are proud of, and are valued above all other activities in the church. This congregation is likely to organise socials, sing 'happy birthday' in services and assume that most people know most people and have a fair bit of knowledge about what is going on in each others lives. Informal, personal connections, and the length people have been in the congregation are at least as important as the formal structures, and perhaps more influential. The church is likely to be run by a network of families and friends who have many ties to the church community.

Boomer and GenX members are comfortable with the 'small is good' mentality of the healthy examples of the family model, which accentuates the value of the individual in community, and the incarnational approach to mission. Belonging might lead to believing and behaving, but numerical growth is seldom a high priority.

Community Model

The community model in some ways incorporates that of the 'family' by valuing the close personal ties and intimate long-standing friendships, whilst also emphasising the shared values of the congregation and wanting to see these reflected in the structures and decision-making processes. Openness and accountability are emphasised, as are opinion-sharing and opportunities for all members to vote and regulate the shared corporate life of the congregation as a community. In terms of mission, priority would be given to ensuring that the programmes of the church, and the charitable action would represent these values on social issues in the wider local area. Involvement in a mission team is a goal rather than a step towards an outcome or action. Involvement in a discussion is an end in itself rather than a means to an end. Civic responsibility and engagement would be esteemed.

You would recognise a 'community' congregation when the eighth notice starts in the service, and perhaps by the joint projects with local charities. This is the model emphasised within GenX, though reformatted to adopt loser non-hierarchical and experimental forms of religious life and worship. You would belong before you believe and would be allergic to legalism and authoritarianism. The teaching would favour discursive styles and discussion-based formats, draw on a fairly wide range of sources, and suggests topical and needs-based discipleship. A thriving small town parish church might tend towards this model.

Leader Model

Excellence in public Worship and teaching would be a high priority in this congregation. The 'leader' congregation would seek to express the values of the members more widely in order to transform the surrounding culture. Focus, energy and resources are given less to providing a context for intimate relationships, although this may be a bi-product, and more to achieving the aims and goals of the church. It is felt that close friendships can be made, but they need to be sought out. The church might value a greater awareness of the 'official' position of the theological tradition, and would tend to look to the church leader to provide clear direction in mission and major decisions. To this congregation the concept of mission would be more activist, and more to do with growing numerically and changing the world, as well as engaging with it or serving it. A 'leader' congregation might expect high levels of buy-in and is likely to enjoy healthy giving as a sign of ownership, active involvement in the ministries of the church and large areas of delegated authority.

Those born in the war years and the NewVics are attracted to 'leader' models of church. They are more likely to be happy to follow clear direction and leadership, and according to Becker, this leads to lower levels of conflict than within any other model.[51] Fellowship is found in doing activities together and pastoral care in small groups. The teaching and preaching might be longer, more didactic in style and would seek to change opinions and call for a response. There would be fewer notices, but lots of them would ask for volunteers! Here you believe in order to belong, in order to behave.

---

51 Becker, pp146-148

Altogether Now... A mixed model of congregation.

The New Victorians, in their desire to appreciate what is old, and to encounter the presence of God want to retain the House of Worship, want to live with close intimate friendships like the family model, be able to share their opinions both within and beyond the congregation and have the social conscience of the 'community', and yet learn how to be leaders, avoid conflict within the congregation and effect change in the world around them. **In other words, expect the Millennials to want it all, and to want it local and global at the same time!**

Previous generations, in attempting a one size fits all haven't attempted an 'all sizes fit all' approach which would best suit the New Vics.

Those of the rising generation who are going to church in large numbers are choosing churches which are able to embrace elements of all the models, with a bias towards 'leader'. This means if the congregation is small, it would have strategic alliances, or a dynamic involvement with a wider movement – if it is larger, it would be broken down into the mid-sized communities beloved of GenX, which in turn are made up of the small groups of the 'family' and have opportunities for large-scale encounters like the 'House of Worship'. They will not want to hear criticisms of other Christians or cultures, and would want to see diversity in the leaders across the sexes and ethnic groups. They are technologically able and will always visit the website of a church before visiting in person, and would like to stay local if they could, but are happy to travel to get what they want in a church. Many, not finding a church which meets all these criteria, might stop going to church regularly without having actually decided to give up their faith.

These observations are not meant to be prescriptive, but we have found them to be helpful.

If you are in a congregation, what type of congregation do you think you are? Has your church gone through cycles or phases in its life where family, or worship, community or leadership have been emphasised? If so, what difference did this make?

God's vision for his Body is expansive, interesting, complex and affirming. What might it take to grow in areas of church life that have been or are being neglected, and would it be possible to pursue ways in which either as a local church, or a movement, a broader vision could emerge? It may be helpful to lay it out like this:

Core task	Congregational Model			
	House of Worship	Family	Community	Leader
Size preference	400 - 2000	20-80	80-300	300+ but ideally over 1000
Generational preference	War years, Boomer, New Vics.	Boomer, GenX	GenX	War years, New Vics.
Worship, Teaching and Discipleship (UP)	Excellence in worship, liturgy, theology of encounter. Few notices.	High level congregational involvement in worship. Personal notices.	High level of congregational involvement in worship and decisions about worship.	High standards in worship music. Excellence in teaching and content. Selected notices.
	Variable approaches to teaching depending on the theological outlook of congregation.	Teaching which assumes shared experience.	Discursive teaching style which avoids assertion and offers opinion.	Well-prepared didactic teaching, aimed at inspiring change.
	God's Word	Our Word of God	Word with God	Word from God.
	Discipleship through classes.	Discipleship through conversations	Subject and needs-based discipleship	Discipleship with courses and study days, which emphasise leadership and team skills.

Fellowship (IN)	Intimacy is possible/individual choice.	Intimacy is paramount. Close, family-like attachments for most/all members.	Close, family-like attachments desirable; for most/all members.	Intimacy is desirable, and resourced through small groups.
	Fellowship through shared worship.	Fellowship through shared experiences	Fellowship through shared opinions.	Fellowship through shared activities
Mission (OUT)	Physical Presence in community is witness, centred around a building.	Existence of the congregation is itself witness,	Express members' values in policies and programmes.	Clearly directed mission aims, goals and ethos.
	The reach is undefined.	The reach is familial.	The reach is local.	The reach is local, regional, even global.
	Mission is 'Come in' to the world.	Mission is 'our love for one another' seen by the world.	Mission is 'salt and light' and engaging in world'.	Mission is proclamation and changing the world.
	Behave to believe to belong.	Belonging might lead to believing and behaving.	Belong before believe.	Believe to belong to behave.

Models and Conflict

Penny Edgell Becker's seminal Sociological work *'Congregations in conflict'* (1999) suggests that conflicts arise when the model of the congregation transitions from one model of congregation into another. Conflict in these circumstances may have little, initially, to do with serious theological or personal disagreements. Many churches, for example, have an endless array of opinions about worship or preaching which happily coexist but if changes threaten the reigning 'model' conflict is likely. In other words if a change seems to some to undermine or alter 'who we are' or a decision seems to have been made in a way contrary to 'the way we do things here' expect the fur to fly.

As a very mild example, our decision as a congregation in London to remove the dilapidated organ from the church building led to negligible conflict within the congregation – I can recall a single complaint letter about process, but a decision to print the annual report in glossy colour led to more 'feedback' – several emails, letters and questions in the Annual General Meeting. The congregation had seldom used the organ in worship, and had adopted a contemporary worship style some time in the

1980's, so removing the organ was to do with creating more space and removing a health hazard and wasn't altering the model of church. Changing the print technique and spending more on the report was deemed to be excessively 'slick and professional' for the ethos of the congregation. In terms of models a transition from 'family' to 'leader' was being signalled by the new approach to the annual report.

SO...

On the face of it the rise of New Victorianism presents an invigorating opportunity for Evangelical Christians, emulating the success of the Great Evangelical Century of their Victorian forebears, but the reality is at present less up-beat. The New Victorians in Britain and the USA are voting with their feet by not attending church. By and large, churches haven't begun to connect because we are still thinking with a GenX mentality (the previous youth culture) when we consider 'younger people'. London appears to be doing less-badly than the rest of the UK, but there is a hugely long way to go to structure and orientate our churches to make them a relevant home and launchpad for the New Victorians. We need to recognise that the post-GenX generations will reject what they perceive to be the errors in those who preceded them just like generations have always done, whilst at the same time retaining other aspects. In other words, how do you rebel against rebelliousness?

In America, Howe and Struass put it neatly: "Will Millennials rebel? Of Course. To predict the timing and nature of their rebellion, lets apply these same rules that worked so consistently for these three earlier generations. As the new youth generation Millennials will reveal themselves as the answers to the central problem facing Xers, the prior youth generation. They will show what can be done about the over-the-top free agency, social splintering, cultural exhaustion and civic decay in an era when Americans are increasingly yearning for community. The Millennial solution will be to set high standards,get organised, team up, and do civic deeds. Millennials will also correct what they perceive are the excesses of middle-aged Boomers – the narcissism , impatience, iconoclasm and constant focus on talk over action. Millennials can do this, over time, by turning towards community, patience, trust, and a new focus on action over talk. *That's* the path by which today's kids can rebel against ageing ex-rebels."[52]

---

52 Howe and Strauss. *Millennials Rising,* p.76

CHAPTER 5

System Sensitive Leadership

If the rising generation known as the Millennials/New Victorians really do substantially differ from the preceding generation we should expect this to impact on the culture and systems of our churches.

That is – if we want to welcome this age group into our churches in any significant number we are going to have to be willing to embrace some of the way they like to operate in our own systems rather than trying to force them into "the way we have always done things here." This is a mission imperative and on the surface seems entirely rational, obvious and easy to achieve. But upon closer inspection it may be costly – even painful.

We have discovered that the causes of conflict in many churches can be explained by a system clash. People operating as they always have, often fail to appreciate that they are perpetuating a system as much as anyone trying to bring in changes is proposing a new system. Are we willing to evaluate and let go of some of our 'ways of doing things here" for the greater cause of welcoming in new people and in particular the New Victorians?

Examining the Operating Systems

Computers provide us with a helpful illustration of how our church might be operating. Computers work on the basis of a combination of hardware, operating systems and software. The New Victorians, who have never known a time without a computer are used to thinking in these kinds of categories. When we apply the same differentiation of computer to church we might get:

Models of church describe the hardware by saying 'who we are'. Are we a PC or a Mac? Are we a new church or an old church, what size and specifications do we have, what tradition or denomination do we belong to?

Operating Systems are ways of answering 'the way we do things'. Are we using Windows, Linux or Leopard. How do we make decisions, what is our attitude to authority or conflict, the role of finance and accountability? Do we meet in small groups mid-week?

Software is 'the ministries'. Are we surfing the

web with Explorer, Firefox or Safari? What about our worship, preaching and teaching, and projects in the local communities? When we are in our small groups – what do we do, how do we study, pray for one another, worship?

Many church leaders and individual Christians make the leap in their thinking direct to the ministries - or the outcomes, without paying enough attention to either 'who we are' or 'how we do things'. Anyone who has transitioned from a PC to a MAC, for example, or between different mobile phones – say a Blackberry to an iPhone, will have to have mastered different techniques, different ways around the system even though in the end the computer or the mobile phone essentially is designed and operated to do the same thing – make phone calls, write emails, look at pictures, surf the internet. It is the same with our churches – as we think about change and growth we need to factor in not just the outcome but the impact on "who we are" and "how we do things" too.

What is a system?

Every person has a system or a number of systems within which they operate in life. These would include their worldview, mindset or paradigm. Some values and ideas have been absorbed or assumed, some learned, others spurned, and some are borrowed for a season. This rag-bag of ideas, values, practices and instinct could be called a system. When we exist alongside others some sense of shared system develops as well. One congregational studies expert writes: *"When people live in community they share a complex pattern of human relationships and interaction develops and this provides the necessary cohesiveness, trust and, as such, a corporate culture in the group."* [53] Churches and congregations have their own operating systems, and so do individuals, societies and work environments. These determine and affirm how we get things done best.

"From its specific worldview and compelling drive each system develops a hierarchy of values and outlooks. The hierarchy then determines what the system pursues by way of aims, rewards and standards of personal conduct." [54]

The hierarchy of values learned and absorbed through education, employment, and previous church experience are more influential for us than we like to admit.

---

53 Hendriks, J, *Studying congregations in Africa,* p.55
54 Ibid.

As we write today we perceive at least 3 operating systems prevalent in many people's work lives which have an impact on their local churches and congregations: the 'organisational', the 'progressive' and the 'entrepreneurial'. Each of these systems can be found upon closer inspection in different churches. Some churches maybe more bureaucratic and efficient, some highly deconstructed or committee focused and still others flying by the seat of their pants behind a bold vision. One generation will chime more closely with each operating system – there will of course be exceptions and crossover, but there are certain general trends which can be usefully observed.

Organisational
80's businesses and some limited contemporary public sector (Chimes with the Boomers)
- authority is essentially hierarchical, power needs harnessing
- tyranny is necessary occasionally but often inefficient
- consultation is research looking for evidences
- organisationally hierarchical
- excellence is found in measurable goals
- risk is managed
- few social programmes
- social theory not so important
- truth is knowable and testable

- pragmatism trumps theory
- characterised by large numbers of employees, many of whom will have a significant focus on administration.

Progressive

90's businesses and contemporary public sector (chimes with X-ers)

- authority is essentially plural
- consultation is an end in itself
- tyranny is avoided at all costs, power needs watering down
- decision-making processes are regularly reformatted, reassessed and published
- excellence is found in process over and above results
- 'view from the middle' is preferable to 'view from above'
- social theory borrows from Marx
- organisationally conservative
- risk averse
- truth is a perspective
- communitarian and project-based social programmes

Entrepreneurial

OO's and dotcom
(chimes with Millennials/New Vics)

- authority is essentially personal and is good

- consultation is a sounding board
- excellence speaks for itself
- vision leads to reality
- organisationally 'flat'
- risk-taking
- process arises out of and serves success
- truth gives you an edge
- teams achieve
- ethical business and fairtrade

Industrialisation, urbanisation and globalisation have played their part in increasing the pace of change in society. This means that the safety that is found from living in and with a community with shared fundamental assumptions is retreating in the face of bewildering complexity.

Our current situation, especially if we are living in urban settings, is that systems jostle. They jostle in our schools and local areas, our universities, cities and in our churches, and different generations find greater affinity with different collections of shared approaches to the world, the self, society and the church.

It is crucial that we become comfortable with the interplay and multiplicity of different ways of understanding, coping with and changing the world in which we live, and that church leaders become adept at leading within complexity. As one leader quipped "I've had to become adept and adapting."

"A prestigious institution provides status, security and established operational procedures, but a fledgling movement is a dynamic, changing, explorative organism that requires a radically different temperament, new motivational drives and a wider range of skills. By definition, movements "move" and therefore requires leaders who are not stuck and insecure when it comes to change and adaptation." [55]

To use the analogy of computers again – we need to branch out from Windows without forgetting how Windows works! Leadership needs to learn to become adept across several platforms, and comfortable working within and around the strength and weaknesses of different approaches.

Hendricks again: *"Systems conflict is a reality. In a globalised world, diversity and pluralism are realities that can no longer be avoided. Homogenous churches usually are single-system churches. To exist in such a church may be the most peaceful, but does not prepare one to live and worship in a world teeming with diversity. The moment that a single system church becomes a multi-system church, diversity and conflict take place, because the way people learn, organise and are led (or want to be led), worship,*

55 Gibbs, *Leadership Next*, p.57

need and expect etc. begins to differ. " [56]

As the progress of the decades shows, the newer generation will generally seek to redress the missed opportunities presented by the inefficiencies or errors of what went before in the market place, politics, education and the media. New entrepreneurial companies have to stay ahead of the curve in order to stay in the game. Bigger companies and bureaucracies watch all of this and adopt or buy up what works once the risk has been taken by others. Competing systems actually co-exist in the world and the workplace, and are in tension with one another for influence and control. We should not be surprised then that similar challenges are presented to local churches who are trying to reach all the generations.

Church life reflects this dynamic nationally and globally, and also within the life of a single congregation. As single-culture churches with single systems of shared 'how we do things' become confused, so this can lead if we are not careful either to conflict or apathy.

Lets take the example of decision-making through taking questionnaires.
• to the organisational, the questionnaire

---

56 Hendriks, J. p 64

responses would check the effect of policy,
- to the progressive, the questionnaire responses should set policy,
- to the entrepreneurial, the questionnaire responses enable a conversation about policy.

Or what about leadership in the church?
- To the organisational, leadership is unambiguous, hierarchical and is usually exercised by people with more years of life experience.
- To the progressive, leadership is corporate and plural (will often involve committees).
- To the entrepreneurial, leadership inspires teams through vision, relationship and observable results.

The key issue is that different systems have different standards of excellence, different hierarchies and produce completely different expectations in the people they serve. We should not expect these ways of operating to be particularly aware or appreciative of the other ways of operating. As one system usually emerges to overcome the failings in another, it is the preceding system which becomes the most frustrating. Hence Gen X struggle to escape the clutches of Boomer bureaucratic and organisational bias and the New Victorians are switched off by the Gen X suspicion of visionary leadership and desire for committees/working groups and discussions as ends in themselves.

When conflict occurs around these issues then we should not be surprised. A first step in navigating our way through this is to accept the fact that each of us is invoking a system of some sort – it is not only the person or group I disagree with who should scrutinize their operating system but myself and the group I identify with. Furthermore, within the church where we are trying to reach those who are outside of our community and may be of a different generation or operating system than our preferred option we have to take a long hard look at our systems and open them up to others, welcoming fresh blood and being prepared to sacrifice our own way of doing things if it will enable us to be a multi-generational church and in particular a church that can engage the New Victorians.

What Might a Millennial-Friendly Church Prioritise?

In his book "Leadership Next" Eddie Gibbs makes it clear that the rising generation are looking for particular qualities and characteristics in their church leaders.[57] He suggests 8 attitudes which he believes are indispensable:

- "A lively intellectual curiosity: an interest in everything- because everything really is related to everything else and therefore to what we are trying to do, whatever it is.
- A genuine interest in what other people think and why they think that way which means you have to be at peace with yourself for a start.
- A feeling of special responsibility for envisioning a future that is different from a straight-line projection of the present. Trends are not destiny
- A hunch that most risks are not there to be avoided but to be taken.
- A mindset that crises are normal, tensions can be promising and complexity is fun.
- A realization that paranoia and self-pity are reserved for people who do not want to be leaders.
- A sense of personal responsibility for the general outcome of your efforts.
- A quality I call "unwarranted optimism" – the conviction that there must be some more upbeat outcome than would result

---

57 Harlan Cleveland cited in Gibbs, Leadership Next, p.57

from adding up all the available expert advice."

We believe that a church with a high impact amongst Millennials will take their preferences and concerns to heart.

Hardware "Who are we?"

The Millennials/New Victorians when surveyed have responded with a resoundingly positive appreciation of big church (by which congregational studies mean at least 200+ although we believe that 500+ is the preference.) It does not follow that this generation are not interested in close relationships within the church though, because they overwhelmingly expect to be part of a small group or mid sized community within the church where they can grow as well. The New Victorians want to feel that they are part of a wider movement – whilst maintaining a focus on the local. Networks of churches with shared values and a place to gather will become increasingly important – with these networks stretching from the local to the global with ease.

Operating System "The way we do things"

A New Victorian-friendly church will be vision
led, involving fluid movements of people and
resources around the church, confident use of
technology, comfortable with a high turn over of
talent, and may well have quick responsive
decision making with a trust in authorized
leadership. Because of the job market they find
themselves in Millennials want to find their
place quickly in the church, get on and serve so
that after a year when they may have to move on
they can have really contributed significantly to
the life of the church. There are likely to be few
committees – with a higher reliance on the skills
of gifted individuals working in teams rather
than dependence on elected bodies of the
chattering classes. In our London church sorting
out a virtually derelict building and site
involved the congregation giving incredibly
generously and trusting a small number of
individuals to oversea getting the agreed works
done. No buildings committee or any other
"project" committee has ever really delivered
visible outcomes. These have been achieved by
empowered Millennials and others working
with their talents to get things done. Millennials
are quite reluctant to fill in many forms - this is
not a lack of commitment as volunteering and
small group membership are high priorities.

These are facilitated by word of mouth, social networking site "groups" and text messaging. For example small groups gain new members by inviting people on Sundays personally or being approached by new people who have chosen them from a list there is not a central bureaucratic allocation system. The New Victorians demonstrate a greater desire to be deployed in service rather than choose a ministry area. This means that proactive ministry leadership is required to go out and invite people to get involved.

A Millennial friendly church will often have strong design concepts and follow these through in all communication – ideally with local talent who understand the church and its locality. A clear unifying "voice" in all media – will be immediately appreciated and recognisible to the New Victorians. The Millennials want to love their church – they are happy with vulnerability but loathe negativity. They will instinctively want to support the leader rather than call everything he/she does into question all the time.

Software "Ministry Outcomes"

Do not expect one mission activity for a church

to satisfy the New Victorians – they want it all: justice, poverty relief, proclamation, discipleship, 24-7 prayer.

A New Victorian friendly church will take preaching seriously – sermons will be thoughtful, inspiring, biblical and practical. Preaching should be passionate and considered with a depth of thought, containing pastoral insight and sensitivity, humour but not frivolity, openness to the leading of the Holy Spirit and practical application. The New Victorians are not looking for theological innovations or speculations.

The preached word will occupy a significant place and length in the main church meeting and New Victorians will often be found notebook in hand wanting to learn and grow!

The New Victorians want to grow as Christians – they take the idea of holiness seriously – not limiting it to traditional piety but wanting relational and ethical morality to shape their daily lives. They are not particularly keen on Gen X style "boundary pushing" with swearing in church or Christians talking about getting drunk. To them this is passé and not what they are about. They long for genuine community and appreciate a church which works at diversity - colour, age, gender and socio –

economic. A New Victorian –friendly church will be sensitive to these cultural priorities, but for many this does not come naturally and will have to be explicitly prioritized by the leadership.

The Millennials also want to have a lot of fun together – they are not as earnest as they sound and do not take themselves too seriously. They may well enjoy doing things together (be it social action, running a marathon, climbing a mountain, learning a new skill together, knitting, pilates or whatever)– and building relationships around causes rather than hanging out with no other purpose in mind. ,

A Millennial friendly church will also prioritise sung worship – valuing the profound joy of worshipping God together and having no fear of intensity in worship. This kind of church will also aspire to see young leaders (including children and teenagers leading their peers) fully released to minster regardless of their age truly responsible for their defined ministry area and with hard working reliable loyal team members gathering around leaders as they emerge.

CHAPTER 6

Wolves and Worms: Threats to the New Victorian Church

Frog, was sitting at a lunch, talking about our congregation, and especially about how young adults enjoyed making decisions, looked for growth in responsibility, loathed committees and had a sense of membership shown through involvement. The other church leaders all had children within the age group we were discussing. Around the table there was a sense of agreement that what he was describing was very different from the way their churches currently ran, organised themselves, but that it would suit their children better. One wise man leant over, looked me in the eye, and said – 'But what are the weaknesses?' 'In my experience', he said, 'often within the greatest strengths lie the greatest weaknesses'. He was not asking me to talk about the normal sins which dog christians and churches, for he was used to expecting those, no, he was asking what in particular might need to be looked out for. Some of the threats to the New-Victorian-friendly church are obvious, some more subtle. Frog's answer was short then, mentioning three things – **vulnerability, leadership, structures.**

Of Wolves and Worms and the Web Generation...

As Paul spoke to the Ephesian church leaders or elders before heading off on his way he warned: 'watch out for the wolves'.

Acts 20: 28-31 *"Keep watch over yourselves and all the flock of which the Holy Spirit has made you overseers. Be shepherds of the church of God, which he bought with his own blood. I know that after I leave, **savage wolves will come in among you** and will not spare the flock. Even from your own number men will arise and distort the truth in order to draw away disciples after them. So be on your guard!"*

The Ephesian church was vibrant, strong and growing, thriving in its urban environment and flourishing in a potent religious culture. It had a good experience of the Holy Spirit (Acts 19:6) a strong grounding in the scriptures through the teaching ministry of Paul in the Hall of Tyrannus over 3 years, an experience of revival as people immersed in the occult came to Christ, and had even dealt with riots and persecution. Furthermore the church Paul addressed had leadership in place ready to take things to the next level, and yet they still had to be on their guard, alert for potential dangers.

2 Timothy 3: 2-7 gives another stark warning to 'watch out for the worms':

*"People will be lovers of themselves, lovers of money, boastful, proud, abusive, disobedient to their parents, ungrateful, unholy, without love, unforgiving, slanderous, without self-control, brutal, not lovers of the good, treacherous, rash, conceited, lovers of pleasure rather than lovers of God— having a form of godliness but denying its power. Have nothing to do with them. They are the kind who **worm their way into homes** and gain control over weak-willed women, who are loaded down with sins and are swayed by all kinds of evil desires, always learning but never able to acknowledge the truth."*

Both the wolves and the worms get 'within' and from there create havoc.

Worms

There is a parallel to be drawn with the rise of the internet. Many aspects of this invention were developed with the intention of spreading information freely and without restriction – to break down the walls of injustice and inequality through quick, effective and cheap transfer of opinions and information. To the New Victorians life without web browsing is not only hard to imagine, it has seldom been lived, and two days offline can lead to withdrawal symptoms and anxiety – a bit like placing someone in solitary confinement. However, though the web offers this fluidity and freedom, it also leaves the doors open and vulnerable to the unscrupulous. Whether the pest is spam offering cut-price medical enhancements or a scam inheritance from a long-lost relative, emails designed to lure people towards pornography sites or even the more ominous predators who pretend to be what they are not and groom children. The freedom leaves both the child and adult on the other side vulnerable by attacking from within the private space between the browser and the screen. Many older adults are decidedly uncomfortable by the levels of self-disclosure which have become normal – tweeting and status updates which tell the world how you are feeling, where you are going, what you are doing – the private world of conversations is laid out, sometimes for the entire world to see, or for several hundred 'friends' to comment upon within a social network. Young adults are seldom bothered by this realm of vulnerability and can feel 'more themselves' when chatting online than in other more traditional social settings.

Computers, especially when they become networked, have both their potential and their vulnerability multiplied. A virus within a computer system, like in organisms and bodies, can self-replicate and spread, infecting the whole through the very channels which are designed to transmit and transport life. The industry and language which has developed to describe all the ways things can go wrong is now bewildering – spyware, malware, Trojans, rootkits, and yes – worms. Computer worms are self-replicating programmes which move across the network rather than concentrating on individual computers or infecting specific files. **Worms spread by exploiting vulnerabilities in operating systems.**

Ness Shroff, Ohio Eminent Scholar in Networking and Communications at Ohio State University, and his colleagues describe the most virulent kind of worm: the kind that scans the Internet randomly, looking for vulnerable hosts to infect.

"These worms spread very quickly," Shroff said. "They flood the Net with junk traffic, and at their most benign, they overload computer networks and shut them down." Code Red was a random scanning worm, and it caused $2.6 billion in lost productivity to businesses worldwide in 2001. Even worse, Shroff said, the worm blocked network traffic to important physical facilities such as subway stations and 911 call centers. "Code Red infected more than 350,000 machines in less than 14 hours. We wanted to find a way to catch infections in their earliest stages, before they get that far," Shroff said.[58]

Paul's comment to Timothy was about worm-like individuals seeking to gain undue control over vulnerable members of the church. There seems to have been a specific local problem here about naïve or suggestible individuals, perhaps those who liked a bit of showbiz and razzmatazz and were more likely to believe anything than to believe nothing. Perhaps people schooled in the spirituality of magic-laden Ephesus couldn't quite wean themselves off their former way of life, leaving their minds and wills susceptible to the kind of 'worm' Paul warns of. I think there are several parallels for the situation we may find ourselves in. Generation Y and younger, happy with spirituality, whose childhood was influenced by Harry Potter stories and a growing fascination with the occult, who have rejected the hard and fast rules of the modernist era, and yet who are not cynical and dismissive of new ideas, are more likely to be taken in by false teachers who prey upon their trust. The very qualities of trust, fluidity and hope are the open doors into house, home and heart which leave

---

58 In June 2008 issue of IEEE Transactions on Dependable and Secure Computing.
http://newswise.com/articles/view/541456/ (accessed 19/03/2010)

them vulnerable.

Wolves

But what about wolves. Wolves are those who pray on the flock. In churches, these are those who stray into dominating rather than releasing, who terrorise and terrify the sheep and make them more cautious and anxious than they already are. They are the enemies of creativity and equality, looking to retain position and role. In a church leadership it will be those threatened by young people leading and making decisions and having responsibility. Most worryingly wolves are already in congregations (from your own number), and in some positions of influence and leadership (arise), but are wanting more (draw away disciples). *'Even from your own number men will arise and distort the truth in order to draw away disciples after them.'* Wolves are not immediately obvious, can be cunning, good analysers of the flock, pleasant to talk to – most disciples are not drawn away by openly unpleasant people. But three things are clearly identified – firstly in the fruit of their ministry there is something destructive and contrary to the Spirit of God, secondly they are distorters or twisters of clear scriptural theology and doctrines, and thirdly they are drawing people away from the whole and towards themselves.

Paul says we have to be 'on our guard'. And so, Frog had to reply to his kind interrogator that the fluid and open network of ideas, individuals and activities which so define a church friendly to Millennials makes them both extraordinary in their entrepreneurial capabilities, and in need of a shepherds who can take on wolves. Bold pastoral ministry will have to develop from within as well as from above for the Millennial's church. Accountability with freedom is a challenging aim, some are so hands off as to be reckless, some so hands on as to be controlling. Some honest people stray into wolf-like attitudes, seeing a church 'out of control' want to reassert order – either by regularising and systematising the holy 'chaos' form above, or by manipulatively 'managing up' . The goal of the Spirit-led church is neither manipulation nor domination but freedom, responsibility and trust.

Our experience of leading and pastoring young adults is by no means exhaustive, but we would love to suggest something more about the nature of shepherding the hearts of today's young adults. We have found a happiness with leadership, a rebirth of leadership and of trust even of large corporations and the ability to change curent social and business trajectories. "Most Millennials are far more trusting than their parents about the capacity of large national institutions to do the right thing on their (and the nation's) behalf." [59]

Leadership starts younger, involves more people, and is fluid and experimental. Todays young adults are looking to take leadership opportunities early – from school age their education has encouraged them to have goals, to handle group exercises and to undertake tasks as a group. Everyone gets a go at leadership, and expects to have a go at developing and growing throughout their journey through life and adulthood. Among the parlance of youth workers and educationalists this 'peer-led' group dynamic is already accepted as best practise, but few youth-workers have managed to translate this into adult church concepts of leadership. But today's young adults are yesterday's youth and they still think, process and lead in similar ways. They are used to delegated authority, expect to be *given* it, and don't expect to have to fight, manoeuvre or even vote for it. Authority isn't won, it is awarded, and it rises from quality relationships, trust and emotional security.

Millennials are happy to lead, and to lead early, through their teenage years but need a sense of security and backing. Some business leaders

59   Strauss and Howe, Millennials rising, p.175

have called this 'narcissism' or 'entitlement', lamenting the naivete of the 'trophy kids', though many others have taken this new paradigm on board and are beginning to realise that workplaces are being transformed and have therefore incorporated teamwork into their decision-making and into their strategies for business achievement. New leaders are looking for real responsibility, but are expecting to have mentors to fall back on, pick up the pieces, open doors and hand-over responsibility.

Here we are presented with a challenge for many churches:
- are we equipped to launch younger leaders before everyone agrees they are 'ready'?
- are we comfortable with a model of development of the life of the church which is open and fluid?

Millennials and Church

"The decline (in church attendance) has happened because more and more adults never started attending in the first place." [60]

"Even if young people want to go to church, the generational decline in church attendance means that

60 David Voas, Quadrant, November 2005.

there is a shortage of adults with the necessary knowledge and skills to accommodate them." [61]

When writing this we were kindly lent some research commissioned for a major global brand, which was trying to help the marketeers place the brand into the psyche of the Millennials. The research suggested that the 'inner circle' of brands (which included Google, Apple and Sony) had become successful at either being:

Trusted	**Agile,**
Transparent	**Engaging**

Conversely it follows that those which were falling out of favour were those thought to be

Untrustworthy	**Stuck**
Secretive or obscure	**Boring**

We believe that one of the fundamental reasons that the Millennials have, by and large, voted with their feet by abandoning church attendance, and perhaps a Christian faith altogether is that as they have grown up, experiencing a new world, connected and transparent through new technologies and a social technology boom which places private lives into the public sphere in a way which shocks their predecessors, while churches appear

---

61 Making Sense of Gen Y, p.14

stuck and obscure, the opposite of fluid, engaging and transparent. Add to this a church environment which seems unconvinced of justice, social fairness and rebuilding communities, and Millennials often never imagine that the answers to the problems of the world could be found in the gospel.

"Only 18% of 18-29 year olds attend religious services every week... The number of college freshmen who named no religious preference doubled between 1985 and 2003. Many young people abandon organized religion because of the restrictive rules it often imposes.." [62]

We are convinced, however, that the essential nature of christian discipleship has more in common with these four positive values than with many of the expressions of church that we have grown up with. Who would not want to worship a God who has a vision for the home and community built on trust, transparency, agility and engagement?

There is an urgency and an opportunity so deep and exciting that it drives us to our knees and to action in equal measures.

What if we could recapture our energy and excitement for the cause of Christ, could allow

62 Twenge, *Generation Me*, p.24

the bold hopes and raw, ridiculous dreams to come into the sight of God again, and make ourselves and our churches ready and available? What if we placed issues of church governance at the bottom of the pile of priorities and allowed discipleship and releasing leadership throughout the body of Christ to rise to the top?

What if, rather than telling younger leaders that they had to choose between the virtues they hold dear, we allowed them to spend themselves for the causes which would take a lifetime to tackle?

What if, despite the broken homes and struggles with sex and addiction, we were able to offer love, support and encouragement to younger men and women as 'works in progress' and still offer them a share in adventure?

What if we take a generation unplugged from God the Father and invite them to reconnect with Christ and the power of the Holy Spirit so they could truly live?

Then, we firmly commend to you the Millennials, the New Victorians, Generation Y and those who come after them – they are not the future church, they are today's church with a hopeful future.

And we will leave you stirring and challenging words from one missionary pioneer of an earlier era, C.T. Studd:

HEROISM is the lost chord; the mission note of present-day Christianity! Every true soldier is a hero! A SOLDIER WITHOUT HEROISM IS A CHOCOLATE SOLDIER! Who has not been stirred to scorn and mirth at the very thought of a Chocolate Soldier! In peace true soldiers are captive lions, fretting in their cages. War gives them their liberty and sends them, like boys bounding out of school, to obtain their heart's desire or perish in the attempt. Battle is the soldier's vital breath! Peace turns him into a stooping asthmatic. War makes him a whole man again, and gives him the heart, strength, and vigour of a hero.

EVERY TRUE CHRISTIAN IS A SOLDIER--of Christ--a hero "par excellence"! Braver than the bravest--scorning the soft seductions of peace and her oft-repeated warnings against hardship, disease, danger, and death, whom he counts among his bosom friends.

THE OTHERWISE CHRISTIAN IS A CHOCOLATE CHRISTIAN! Dissolving in water and melting at the smell of fire. "Sweeties" they are! Bonbons, lollipops! Living their lives on a glass dish or in a cardboard box, each clad in his soft clothing, a little frilled white paper to preserve his dear little delicate constitution.

BIBLIOGRAPHY

American Demographics. *Getting Inside Gen Y-Generation Y.* September 1, 2001. http://findarticles.com/p/articles/mi_m4021/is_2001_Sept_1/ai_78426787/ (accessed October 26, 2009).

Anderson, Janna Quitney. *Future of the Internet III: How the Experts See It.* December 14, 2008. http://pewresearch.org/pubs/1053/future-of-the-internet-iii-how-the-experts-see-it (accessed November 30, 2009).

Barna Group. *New Research Explores the Long-Term Effect of Spiritual Activity among Children and Teens.* 2009. http://www.barna.org/barna-update/aticle/15-familykids/321-new-research-explores-the-long-term-effect-of-spiritual-activity-among-children-and-teens (accessed November 10, 2009).

BBC News. *UK Youths 'Among Worst in Europe'.* November 2, 2006. http://newsvote.bbc.co.uk/mpapps/pagetools/print/news.bbc.co.uk/l/hi/uk/6108302.stm (accessed October 20, 2009).

Bennett, Jim, and Dixon, Mike. "Single Person Households and Social Policy." *Joseph Rowntree Foundation.* 2006. http://www.jrf.org.uk/sights/files/jrf/bennett-9781859354759.pdf (accessed December 12, 2009).

Bunch, Jim, Fields, Bea, Newbold, Rob, and Wilder, Scott. *Millennial Leaders: Success Stories from Today's Most Brilliant Generation Y Leaders.* Buffalo Grove, IL: Writers of the Round Table Press, 2008.

Campbell, W. Keith, and Twenge, Jean M. *The Narcissism Epidemic.* New York: Free Press, 2009.

Carson, D.A. *Becoming Conversant with the Emerging Church.* Grand Rapids, Michigan: Zondervan, 2005.

CBS News. *The "Millennials" are Coming.* May 25, 2008. http://www.cbsnews.com/stories/2007/11/08/60minutes/main3475200.shtml?tag=contentMain;contentBody (accessed December 15, 2009).

Chansanchai, Athima. *'Millennials' Lead the Wired Life.* September 6, 2006.
http://www.msnbc.msn.com/id/14560871/ (accessed December 2, 2009).

Erickson, Tamara. *Plugged In: The Generation Y Guide to Thriving at Work.* Boston, MA: Harvard Business Press, 2008.

Facebook. *Statistics/ Facebook.* January 10, 2010.
http://www.facebook.com/press/info.php?statistics (accessed January 10, 2010).

Fox, Susannah, and Jones, Sydney. "Generations Online in 2009." *Pew/Internet.* January 28, 2009.
http://pewinternet.org/~/media//Files/Reports/2009/PIP_Generations_2009.pdf (accessed December 10, 2009).

Glaser, Mark. *Finding Balance in Teen Use of Social Media.* October 20, 2006.
http://www.pbs.org/mediashift/2006/10/finding-balance-in-teen-use-of-social-media293.html (accessed January 28, 2010).

Godin, Seth. *Tribes: We Need You to Lead Us.* New York: Portfolio, 2008.

Gordon, Bryony. *The New Victorians.* October 7, 2007. http://www.telegraph.co.uk/fashion/stellemagazine/3361713/The-new-Victorians.html (accessed January 20, 2010).

Greenberg, Eric, and Weber, Karl. *Generation We: How Millennial Youth are Taking Over America and Changing the World.* Pachatusan, 2008.

Howe, Neil, and Strauss, William. *The Fourth Turning: An American Prophecy.* New York: Broadway Books, 1997.

Huntley, Rebecca. *The World According to Y: Inside the New Adult Generation.* Crows Nest, NSW: Allen & Unwin, 2006.

Jayson, Sharon. *Gen Y's Goal? Wealth and Fame.* January 10, 2007. http://www.usatoday.com/news/nation/2007-01-09-

gen-y-cover_x.htm (accessed November 3, 2009).

—. *The 'Millennials' Come of Age.* June 29, 2006.
http://www.usatoday.com/life/lifestyle/2006-06-28-
generation-next_x.htm (accessed November 27,
2009).

Keeter, Scott, and Taylor, Paul. "The Millennials."
pewreseach.org. December 11, 2009.
http://pewresearch.org/pubs/1437/millennials-profile
(accessed January 12, 2010).

MarketingVOX. *Millennials Prefer Social
Networking to Internet Porn.* September 17, 2008.
http://www.marketingvox.com/millennials-prefer-
social-networking-to-internet-porn-041007/ (accessed
October 30, 2009).

Martin, Carolyn A, and Tulgan, Bruce. *Managing
Generation Y: Global Citizens Born in the Late
Seventies and Early Eighties.* Amherst, MA: HRD
Press Inc., 2001.

Mousley, Kevin. *Children of Wealth: Rich
Reflections.* October 28, 2008.

http://new.bbc.co.uk/1/hi/business7687171.stm
(accessed December 10, 2009).

Newport, Frank. *Questions and Answers About Americans' Religion.* December 24, 2007.
http://www.gallup.com/poll/103459/Questions-Answers-About-Americans-Religion.aspx (accessed December 3, 2009).

Office for National Statistics. "Health Statistics Quarterly." *www.statistics.gov.uk.* Edited by Alison Wiles Charlie Wroth. April 27, 2009.
http://www.statistics.gov.uk/downloads/theme_population/KPVS34-2007/KPVS2007.pdf (accessed November 2, 2009).

—. "Office for National Statistics."
www.statistics.gov.uk. April 27, 2009.
http://www.statistics.gov.uk/downloads/theme_health/HSQ41.pdf (accessed October 22, 2009).

Pink, Daniel H. *A Whole New Mind: Why right-Brainers Will Rule the Future.* New York: Riverhead Books, 2006.

Raines, Claire. *Managing Millennials.* 2002.
http://www.generationsatwork.com/articles_millennia
ls.php (accessed December 12, 2009).

Rainie, Lee. *Digital 'Natives' Invade the Workplace.*
September 28, 2006.
http://pewresearch.org/pubs/70/digital-natives-invade-
the-workplace (accessed November 30, 2009).

Rosen, Larry, D. *Rewired: Understanding the
iGeneration and the way they learn.* (Palgrave
MacMillan, 2010)

Saad, Lydia. "By Age 24, Marriage Wins Out."
www.gallup.com. August 11, 2008.
http://www.gallup.com/poll/109402/Age-24-
Marriage-Wins.aspx?version=print (accessed
December 2, 2009).

Samuel, Henry. *Modest Young French Women Refuse
to go Topless.* July 22, 2009.
http://www.telegraph.co.uk/news/worldnews/europe/f
rance/5887753/Modest-young-French-women-refuse-
to-go-topless.html (accessed December 8, 2009).

Savage, Sara, Collins-Mayo, Sylvia, Mayo, Bob with Cray, Graham. *Making Sense of Generation Y: The World View of 15-25-year-olds.* London: Church House Publishing, 2006.

Sophia Network. *Let's Hear it for the Boys!* October 12, 2009. http://blog.sophianetwork.org.uk/2009/10/lets-hear-it-for-the-boys.html (accessed December 10, 2009).

Strauss, Neil Howe and William. *Millennials Rising: The Next Generation.* New York: Vintage Books, 2000.

Twenge, Jean M. *Generation Me: Why Today's Young Americans are More Confident, Assertive, Entitled - and More Miserable Than Ever Before.* New York: Free Press, 2007.

UK Youth Research. *UK Tribes Explained.* 2009. http://www.uktribes.com/about (accessed November 14, 2009).

UNICEF. "Child Poverty Report." *www.unicef.org.* 2007.

http://www.unicef.org/media/files/ChildPovertyRepor
t.pdf (accessed October 29, 2009).

US Census Bureau. "Current Population Reports." *US
Census Bureau.* September 13, 2002.
http://www.census.gov/compendia/statab/2010/tables/
10s0007.pdf (accessed November 18, 2009).

USA Today. *Unicef Ranks Well-Being of British, U.S.
Children Last in Industrialized World.* February 14,
2007. http://www.usatoday.com/news/world/2007-02-
14-unicef-child-wellbeing_x.htm (accessed October
23, 2009).

Walker, Kim. "20-30's and the Church: A Statistical
Overview." *www.eauk.org.* 2009.
http://www.eauk.org/theology/upload/20-30s-and-the-
church-A-Statistical-Oveview.pdf (accessed October
25, 2009).

Yan, Sophia. *Understanding Generation Y.* December
8, 2006.
http://www.oberlin.edu/stupub/ocreview/2006/12/08/f
eatures/Understanding_Generation_Y.html (accessed
January 21, 2010).

YouGov.com. "YouGov Survey Results." *www.yougove.co.uk.* January 14, 2008. http://www.yougov.co.uk/extranets/ygarchives/conten t/pdf/DMIRROR_debt_080114.pdf (accessed December 5, 2009).